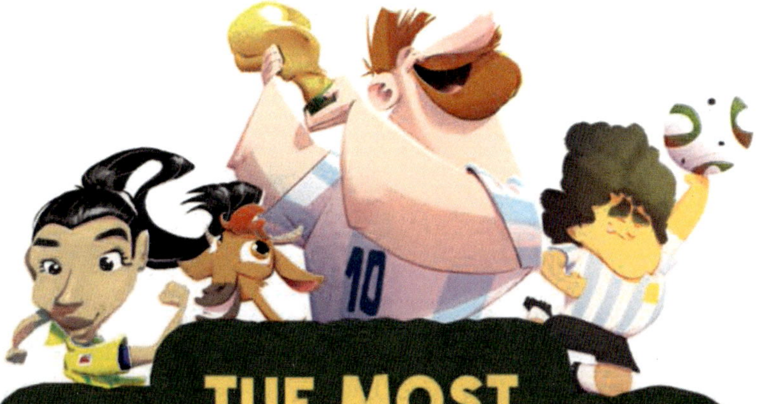

THE MOST

AMAZING SOCCER STORIES

OF ALL TIME

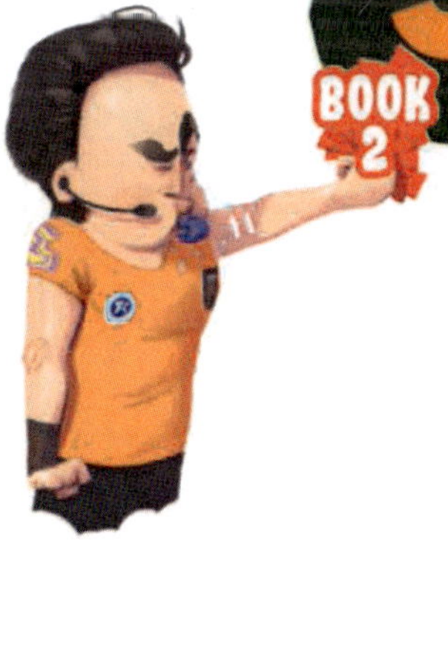

BOOK 2

FOR KIDS

Michael Langdon

@itsmikelangdon

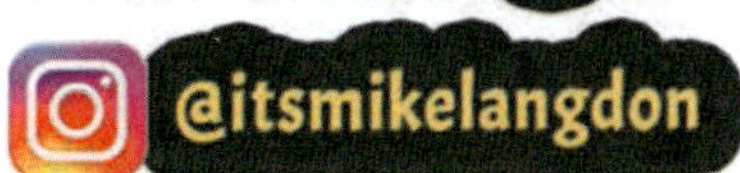

Dedication

To Sarah:

A lifetime of gratitude and love
for supporting my maiden voyage into publishing.

Table of contents

The crowning of The GOAT

Once upon a time, in the land of Qatar, the stage was set for the crowning of the soccer king - The Greatest Of All Time.

Lionel Messi was undoubtedly the best soccer player in the world, but to truly earn the title of The GOAT, he needed to win one specific trophy: The FIFA World Cup.

As his soccer superpowers were starting to wane, the 2022 World Cup was his final chance to win the prestigious event that only comes around once every four years. The weight of 45 million Argentineans rested squarely on his shoulders, and the pressure to perform well was immense.

Despite losing his first match, Messi's talent and perseverance shone through as he went on to score a goal at every stage of the World Cup. He single-handedly carried his team all the way to the final.

The final was the greatest the world had ever seen. The game ended in a 3-3 draw with France, and Messi scored two of the six goals. As the game ended in a draw, it had to be decided on penalties.

Lionel Messi's 20 years of tricks, goals, and mesmerizing dribbles were about to be recognized as the best ever, but only if the last penalty kick went in. His teammate Gonzalo Montiel stood on the penalty spot, and it all came down to that one kick of a soccer ball.

Montiel scored, and Messi, who was in the center circle, collapsed on his knees crying tears of joy. He had finally been crowned as the King of the Soccer World - the undoubted Greatest Of All Time.

10
10

If we're going to talk about the male GOAT, we should also talk about the female GOAT.

(A doe is the name of a female goat in case you were wondering about the name of this chapter 😊)

In women's soccer we have someone who is so incredibly good, so outrageously talented, that she is the undisputed Greatest Of All Time.

Her name? Marta Vieira Da Silva of Brazil - simply known around the world as Marta.

She was the first soccer player of any gender to score at five World Cups, a feat which, in the men's game, has only recently been matched by Cristiano Ronaldo.

Marta is renowned for her grace on the ball, and the ease with which she can glide past any defender that tries to stop her. Watching her is the closest the world has come to actually witnessing poetry in motion.

The greatest accolade that can be given to Marta, on top of her being named Women's Player of the Year a record 6 times, is that she is the best to have ever played despite never winning the World Cup.

A very special mention must be given to the second greatest player of all time: Mia Hamm.

The American forward, who retired in 2004, remains in a class of her own. Most notably because of the decade she had in the 1990s, where she won two World Cups and two Olympic gold medals.

More sendings off than players on the field!

The scenes that followed Argentina's World Cup triumph after Lionel Messi's performance in 2022, showed us that the South American country is full of very passionate soccer people.

Sometimes this passion can be shown in moments of happiness or in moments of frustration.

Unfortunately for the teams of Claypole and Victoriano Arenas, their players were very passionately frustrated after a game in 2011.

After the game against Claypole, Victoriano Arenas players were not happy when the full time whistle was blown, and the mother of all fights broke out in the center circle. And it wasn't just the 22 players on the pitch getting involved.

Not wanting to be left out, along came the substitutes and the coaching staff of both teams to show their frustration.

Legend has it that even the bus drivers of the opposing teams got involved in the action!

In the aftermath of the storm, referee Damian Rubino walked into the dressing room of both teams to individually send off every single member of staff in each team.

That amounted to 36 red cards in total, and a Guinness Book of World Records award for the most sendings off in a single game of soccer!

The smell of disaster

The beautiful game has provided us with many funny tales. Whilst some of them are laugh-out-loud funny, others are peculiar.

Santiago Cañizares of Spain starred in one such tale in 2002. A story many found peculiar, but one that Cañizares himself certainly did NOT find funny.

The Spaniards were going through to the 2002 World Cup as one of the favorites.

Cañizares had just established himself as the Spanish number one goalkeeper, which at 32 years old, was somewhat late.

Whilst in his hotel room, days before flying to the World Cup, he headed into the bathroom to prepare himself for the night. That's when disaster struck!

His teammates heard a commotion from across the hall, and wanting to find out what had happened, they rushed to Cañizares' room only to be stopped by the doctors.

"Don't come in - there's glass everywhere" Doctors told his teammates.

Fearing the worst (like a break-in or an intruder) his teammates were somewhat relieved a few minutes later when they heard the news from the doctors.

It turned out that Cañizares accidentally knocked over a bottle of aftershave that was sitting on the bathroom sink.

The bottle smashed on the floor and broke into lots of tiny pieces and a couple of large shards.

Unfortunately for Spain's number one, one of those large shards flew into his foot and cut it really badly. He missed the World Cup and was out of action for a month.

How is that for the unluckiest injury in the history of the sport?

From an unlucky injury to probably the luckiest soccer player to survive an injury!

In the 1956 FA Cup final, Manchester City were playing Birmingham City at Wembley to decide the English Cup Champions.

With a quarter of an hour to play, a ball was played into City's box and a Birmingham striker nodded it down towards his oncoming teammate.

His teammate would have slotted it into the back of the net had it not been for the goalkeeper Bert Trautmann. Or to be more specific, Bert Trautmann's neck.

The running striker went, knee first, into Trautmann's neck, and whilst the keeper made the save, he lay motionless on the Wembley turf for a good few minutes.

He eventually got up whilst massaging his neck. A bit like when one sleeps at a funny angle and wakes up with a sore neck.

Trauttmann's neck wasn't sore. He had actually broken his neck in 5 places!

Luckily for Trautmann, English treatment for broken necks in the 1950s was world class. The coach rushed onto the pitch and fixed the injury by rubbing a wet sponge all over the keeper's face.

That allowed Trauttmann to keep playing in the game and become an FA Cup winner.

He would go on to collect his winners medal (still clutching his neck as if he'd had a bad sleep) from the Royal Box.

It was only a few days later, after the pain wouldn't go away that he went to the doctor and found out how bad his injury actually was!

The Kaiser

Another superhuman story of grit and resilience through injury (or just pure madness?!) goes to Trautmann's compatriot and one of history's very best players, Franz Beckenbauer. Also known as "The Kaiser".

In a World Cup semi-final game in 1970 he had one of his most incredible games. The game was dubbed "The Game of Century" - purely because it was a 4-3 thriller between two giants of the world game, Germany and Italy.

But on a personal level for Beckenbauer, what he did on the pitch that day defies belief.

After an early challenge by an Italian player, Beckenbauer landed awkwardly on his shoulder and broke his collarbone.

Any normal person would have gone straight to hospital, but not Der Kaiser.

Instead he ordered his medical team to bring a sling onto the pitch.

He placed his broken shoulder into the sling and continued to play for not only 90 minutes, but a whole 120 minutes, as the game went into extra time!

What makes Beckenbauer's performance so incredible is that he produced a masterclass of a display that day

In a world cup semi-final.

With a broken bone.

With his arm strapped to his chest.

In the center of the pitch!

The man, it would seem, was made from steel!

Sportsmanship gone too far

From a man made of steel to a man made of fluffy rainbows and unicorns.

Well, that's absolutely not the way anyone would describe Italian soccer player Paolo Di Canio, but there was one particular moment in his West Ham career that will go down in history.

West Ham were playing Everton and they were desperate for points.

There were 5 minutes left on the clock when an opportunity to clinch the 3 points - which they desperately needed - came West Ham's way.

A long ball was played into the Everton area and their goalkeeper, Paul Gerrard, was first to the ball to half clear it towards the corner flag. As he tried to run towards the ball to ensure it was fully cleared, he collapsed in agony clutching his leg. He had clearly injured himself.

With the keeper out of action 20 meters from his goal, the ball continued rolling towards the corner flag, where a West Ham player found it and fired a first time cross into the area.

The cross was remarkably accurate and heading towards one of the best strikers in the Premier League, Paolo Di Canio.

Di Canio was great at heading, volleying and scoring seemingly difficult goals, so whilst the ball was in the air and heading directly at him - and given that he was unmarked - everyone in that instant knew that it was going to end in the back of the net.

What happened next took everyone by surprise. Di Canio grabbed the ball with his hands and immediately told everyone to stop playing so that the Everton keeper could get some medical assistance.

His teammates were outraged, but the Everton players and fans applauded his selflessness.

To this day it remains one of the greatest fairplay gestures the world has ever seen!

10

The Wonderkid that never was

We've already spoken about Messi in Chapter One. The likes of him and Pelé come round once in a generation. Absolute beasts of the game who have no equals.

In between the eras of Pelé, Maradona and Messi/Ronaldo, there was one kid who was blessed with more natural ability than people had ever seen.

So much so, that he was given a $1 million sponsorship agreement by Nike at 14 years of age. That same year, he broke into the first team of DC United and scored his first professional goal.

All this a few months into becoming a teenager. He really was the real deal!

His name? Freddy Adu.

The American superstar was poised to become the greatest soccer player of all time. Just ask Pele who starred in a few television commercials with the 14 year old.

His progression continued, and at 16, he was training with Manchester United, under the watchful eye of the most successful British manager of all time, Sir Alex Ferguson.

Sadly, he didn't quite turn heads at Manchester United, and his career declined. In the end he never really played for a big club or won any major trophies.

He claims that his failure to reach the dizzying heights he was predicted was because clubs saw him as a marketing tool. It didn't allow him to nurture his talent and focus on his soccer career. However, the story does have a lovely ending.

Having had an unprivileged upbringing, all the money he made as a child went towards financially helping his mom, who had worked a few jobs after emigrating from Ghana to the USA to provide for her family.

Mother Adu never had to work again after Freddy turned 14.

100
100
100

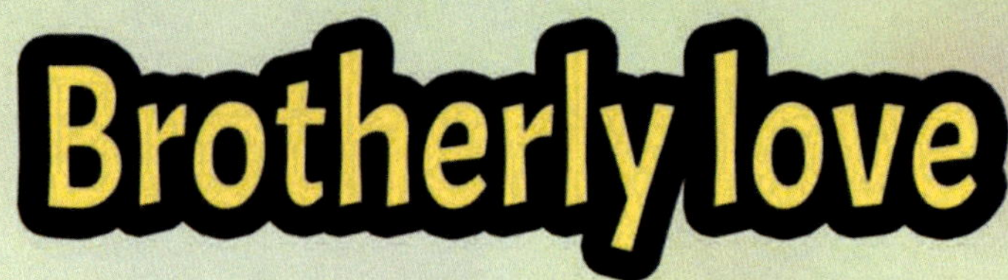

Brotherly love

On June 23 2010 Ghana and Germany met in a World Cup match that made history for a very peculiar reason.

Brothers had often graced World Cup games and produced some real feel good family tales (from the Charlton Brothers winning the World Cup for England through to the De Boers for The Netherlands and the Laudrups for Denmark), but when Jerome and Kevin-Prince Boateng met in Johannesburg in 2010, they made headlines for very different reasons.

They were representing different countries!

Their father, Prince, moved to Germany from Ghana in 1981. A few years later he fathered Kevin-Prince with his first wife. After that marriage failed, he fathered Jerome with his second wife.

Both children would go on to represent Germany in soccer at youth level before Kevin-Prince switched allegiance and chose to represent Ghana. He had been unhappy about being left out of a U21 Germany squad and took the rash decision to change sides.

The two talented soccer players continued to rise through the ranks and play at the peak of the sport – and consequently they were selected by their nations to represent them.

When the draw for the World Cup in South Africa took place, all eyes turned to the Ghana VS Germany game as it would see brothers play against each other for the first time ever in a World Cup.

The game ended in a 1-0 victory to Germany courtesy of a Mesut Özil goal.

Curiously, the brothers would go on to line up against each other again at the following World Cup in Brazil.

Funnily enough, it is said by people close to the brothers, that George Boateng, the pair's older brother, was a much better soccer player than both Kevin-Prince and Jerome. Unfortunately for George, a troubled upbringing derailed his career..

BOATENG
20

A 5 month long game

On November 26 1898 referee Thomas Saywell accidentally blew for full time 10 minutes early in a match between Southampton FC and Millwall FC.

The mistake could not be immediately rectified by the referee as a pitch invasion occurred. So he proceeded to mark the game as over with the scoreline as it was. Millwall were losing so they were not happy about the decision.

So much so that they contested the referee's decision in a tribunal, and demanded that the remaining 10 minutes be played so that they had a fair chance of winning the game.

Nothing too unusual there apart from the fact that Millwall were losing 4-1 and had very little time to draw, let alone win, the match.

After 5 months of debate, the tribunal ruled in favor of Millwall. They decided that the last 10 minutes had to be played before the end of the season.

Southampton were forced to make the 160 mile return journey to London in April 1899 to play the last 10 minutes of a game that they surely had already won. A journey that (over 120 years ago!) must have been hard to make.

Begrudgingly they made their way to The Den to play those last 10 minutes. The result was one of the most incredible comebacks the world of soccer has ever seen....

...not really, those 10 minutes were the most boring 10 minutes of soccer ever seen, and the game still ended up being 4-1 to Southampton.

They went back to the south coast of England feeling like their time had been truly wasted, but at least the scoreline could be made official and Millwall could finally stop their whinging.

1899
1898

The most confusing match ever!

Winning a soccer game is simple: Put the ball in the opposing goal more times than your rival.

The sport becomes less simple when someone comes up with a rule that is so confusing, that it results in two competing teams trying their hardest to score own-goals!

This was the case in 1994, when Barbados and Grenada met in Concacaf's Shell Cup.

In an effort to increase the cup's popularity, the organizers imposed a rule which stated that a Golden Goal scored in extra time would not only win a match, but also count as two goals.

In the semi-final, Barbados needed to win by two clear goals to qualify for the final.

Barbados were leading 2-0 when, with 7 minutes of normal time remaining, Grenada scored to make it 2-1.

Barbados realized that they would be more likely to reach the final if they scored an own goal in the next 7 minutes, and then score a goal (worth two goals) in extra time.

What happened next was farcical: A Barbados defender shamelessly scored an obvious own goal.

The Grenadians realized that they needed one more goal at either end of the field to go through to the final (3-2 would see them win on points whilst 2-3 would see them win on goal difference).

The most unusual 3 minutes ever witnessed in international soccer followed.

Barbadians were defending their own goal as well as that of the opposition – the Grenadians were desperately trying to score at either but had no luck.

The game went into extra time, where Barbados scored the Golden Goal that counted for two. That took them through to the final of the 1994 Shell Cup final.

Third bite of the cherry!

One of the least common offenses seen on a soccer pitch is players biting opponents. So when TV cameras capture three, and all of them are committed by the same player, you've got to question whether the player is simply just hungry!

Luis Suárez's first bite came in 2010 when he was playing for Ajax against PSV. There was a strong challenge in the middle of the pitch, and a small disagreement broke out.

It was during this disagreement that Suarez inexplicably bit Otman Bakkal in the shoulder. The referee missed it so Suarez went unpunished on the day.

However, the TV cameras did capture the incident, and after reviewing the footage, the Dutch Soccer Association suspended Suarez for 7 games.

Three years later, whilst playing for Liverpool FC, there was a coming together between Suárez and Chelsea's Branislav Ivanovic. The Chelsea defender was left rubbing his right arm in agony. Television replays showed that Suarez had taken a bite off of the defender's arm (again!).

Remarkably, this wasn't to be the last time he'd bite an opponent.

The next year he chomped on Giorgio Chiellini's shoulder during a World Cup game between Uruguay and Italy.

The referee again missed the action (he bites quickly!) but the cameras did pick it up.

Suárez claimed he was not responsible for the bite on Chiellini. Apparently he lost his balance and fell, teeth first, into Chiellini's shoulder.

A laughable excuse that makes you wonder whether he used the old " the dog ate my homework" excuse when he was at school.

After that third offense the Uruguayan was banned from all soccer-related activities for 4 months. That must have been hard to swallow.

A fan's dream come true

Steve Davies is an ardent fan of West Ham. And unfortunately for West Ham manager Harry Redknapp, Davies stood right behind his dugout on July 27 1994 when West Ham were playing a friendly game away to Oxford City.

Davies, an amateur soccer player, kept screaming his opinions to Harry Rednkapp on how he should be managing the team. As a matter of fact, he just wouldn't shut up about it, so Redknapp definitely noticed him on the day!

At the stroke of half time, Redknapp found himself a player down and with no available replacements on the bench. So he turned to the man that had been annoying him throughout the whole of the first half.

He strode over to the loud-mouthed fan behind the dugout and said "Oi, can you play as good as you talk?"

Next thing you know, Davies was being hustled down the tunnel to the changing rooms to be kitted out in the Claret & Blue. A few minutes later he came out and played for West Ham.

Davies was living the dream playing for the team he supported – and in the 71st minute it got even better: He scored a goal!

West Ham United went on to win 4-0 with Davies getting on the scoresheet for his boyhood club.

Unfortunately for the Hammers fan, West Ham didn't give Davies a contract.

They wouldn't even let him keep the shirt he played in, as the club needed it for their upcoming game against Newcastle!

11

The Bald Buddha

Some people avoid walking under ladders, others believe a smashed mirror signifies 7 years of bad luck.

Whatever crazy beliefs people may have, they probably don't measure up to the mad superstitions most soccer players have. And it seems to be everywhere in the game!

From wearing the same aftershave to games, the same socks, and rubbing certain players' bellies, we've seen it all on the soccer pitch.

One of the most iconic superstitions comes from the 1998 World Cup, and seemingly a very successful one as they ended up winning the whole tournament.

The superstition came from the French team and its main characters were Laurent Blanc and Fabien Barthez. On the way to World Cup victory, Blanc started a tradition of kissing the bald goalkeeper's head.

After the national anthems were sung, and before kick off, the defender would go over to his goalkeeper, firmly grab his face with two hands, pull the top of his head towards him, and give a kiss on his crown.

Quite the ridiculous theatrics. The only thing is, that the more they did it throughout the tournament, the more they won!

When they reached the final, which Blanc was suspended for, the whole of France was in a panic! How would they beat the Brazilians without that pre-match kiss?

Luckily for the whole nation, just before kick off and still in his tracksuit, Blanc came out of the dugout and kissed the goalkeeper on his head.

The whole of Brazil must have known it signified the impending doom.

Brazil did go on to have a shocker of a game – they lost 3-0 in the final.

The most superstitious of us still know it was all down to that lucky Blanc kiss.

L.BLANC
5

Shin pad superstitions

Shin pads are an important part of the game. First and foremost, they keep players safe - having undoubtedly prevented many broken bones over the years.

Secondly, it would seem, many soccer players use them in superstitious rituals before a game.

England international soccer player Kyle Walker has worn the same shin pads every match day for the last 14 years. The defender, who earns over half a million dollars every month, has not once bought a new pair since he became a professional.

That's over 500 sweaty games that he's been wearing them for. "They will always be there. I will never change them" Walker has said. Apparently they still structurally resemble a shin pad – so they just about provide enough protection to his legs...

Another player who took superstitions to a new level was ex-England captain John Terry, who claimed to have had over 50 pre-match rituals. Much like Kyle Walker, he wore the same shin pads for over 10 years, and was devastated when he once lost them at Barcelona's Camp Nou.

So much so that he nearly had a panic attack thinking that the reason why they were 11 minutes from losing their following game (a cup final against Liverpool) was all down to the lost shin pads.

Terry's other superstitions included listening to the exact same songs every day before a match day and parking in exactly the same spot every time he drove to the stadium. He apparently went crazy for two hours before one particular game, when someone parked in his spot!

Another curious superstition came from Manchester United defender Phil Jones who would put his right sock on first if he was playing a home game and his left sock on first if the game was away.

26

The most disastrous debut

Ask any soccer fan about the worst debut in world history and they'll utter two words: Jonathan Woodgate.

The English defender was bought by Real Madrid from Newcastle in 2004. That's despite his previous season being riddled with injuries. So badly riddled with injuries that Real Madrid would not see him play for the club 13 months after they paid $13 million for him.

A million dollars for every month he laid in the physiotherapist's massage table!

By the time the 25-year-old's debut came, it had been 17 months since he had played soccer. Judging by his actions on the field that day, it looked more like it had been 17 years.

Woodgate must have been picturing a dream debut where he scored. And that's exactly what he did 25 minutes into the game. Unfortunately for Woodgate, it was an own goal!

Things couldn't get any worse for Woodgate... Or could they?

Within a minute of his teammates scoring two goals to counteract the one that Woodgate had scored against them, he got himself sent off!

You could be forgiven for thinking he was purposely trying to sabotage Real Madrid that day.

Madrid's "Galacticos" were made to sweat that day, and they once again saved Woodgate's bacon. They went on to score a third goal and Madrid won the game 3-1.

Woodgate's blushes will probably never be spared, as it's hard to imagine a worse debut for a club of that magnitude.

He never managed more than three appearances in a row for Real Madrid and went back to England, to the modest Middlesbrough FC, at the end of his maiden Spanish season.

siemens

The Hand of God

In 1986 England and Argentina met in the World Cup. Tensions were still running high from a war they had fought 4 years earlier.

The game was a knock-out quarter final game and two of the most remarkable things in World Cup history happened over the course of the following 90 minutes.

In the first half, a young Diego Maradona waltzed around the English back line before trying to play a one-two with his team mate. Maradona was so good that he got the English defender to play the one two for him - the defender accidentally looping the ball into the 6 yard box.

English goalkeeper Peter Shilton was just about to punch the ball away, when the little Argentinian magician jumped up and used his hand to nudge the ball into the back of the net.

An illegal move that was so audacious in nature that everyone in the ground was wondering why he was crazy enough to celebrate it like he was.

The problem was that the referee didn't spot the infringement and allowed the goal to stand.

Maradona didn't wait too long to admit his guilt. After the match he said it wasn't his hand that scored the goal, but rather "the hand of God".

To make matters worse for the English, four minutes later Maradona danced his way around half a dozen English players before slotting the ball past the English goalkeeper.

It was one of the most beautiful sights global soccer has ever seen. True poetry in motion. It became known as "The Goal of the Century".

It was something for the Argentineans to celebrate after a decade of disagreements with the English.

Winning a tournament they didn't qualify for!

At the end of June 1992 the Danish National side were flying back to Denmark with the Euro '92 trophy. But they had not even qualified to be there!

10 days before the tournament was due to start, Yugoslavia got disqualified because of international conflict. The Danes, who had come second in Yugoslavia's qualifying group, got catapulted into a group that contained Sweden, France and England.

Everyone (Danes included) thought they were there quite literally to fill an empty space left by the Yugoslavians. They drew against England in the first game.

Their second game saw them lose to Sweden, after which, the TV commentator famously said "Denmark are out of the European championship, how awful is that?".

The commentator was simply not expecting the Danes to beat the French team and the Swedes to beat World Cup semi-finalists England. And That's exactly what happened

Denmark were then up against The Netherlands, winners of the last European Championship. A side containing an almost incredible mix of legends of the game and upcoming talent.

The names of Rijkaard, De Boer, Koeman, Gullit, Bergkamp and Van Basten stood between Denmark and a place in the final. The game went to a penalty shootout after ending 2-2.

Danish goalkeeper Peter Schmeichel decided he was going to dive left for the first penalty in the shootout. Regardless of who was taking the first penalty.

Schemeichel became a world legend that day. He saved a penalty from Marco Van Basten and took his team to the final.

Denmark then beat giants Germany 2-0 in the final. The Danish minnows, who hadn't even qualified for the tournament, had just created history by winning Euro 1992.

Brazil's greatest humiliation

Brazilians, it seems, are born naturally being super talented at soccer.

Generation after generation they have thrived on the international stage, being the most successful team in the history of the sport with 5 World Cups.

So when they were playing at home in the semi-final of the 2014 World Cup - it was inevitable that they'd progress to the final. Then again, the Germans ain't bad at soccer either.

What Germany did to Brazil on the evening of July 8 2014 in Mineirão was torture.

They killed the joy of 200 million people. The collective happiness of a country sapped out of them in 90 fateful minutes.

Neither Germany nor Brazil had dropped a point on their way to the semi-finals. And the Brazilians were favorites to win the tournament given they were playing on home turf.

When the game kicked off, Brazil were quick off the traps and got a corner after 37 seconds. That would be as good as it got for them.

Before the half hour, Müller, Klose, Kroos (twice) and Khedira had put Germany 5-0 up. In scoring that goal, Klose overtook Ronaldo as the leading World Cup scorer in history.

Ronaldo himself was watching in the stands - talk about adding salt to the wound!

Schürrle scored another brace before full time to make it 7-0.

Poor old Oscar dos Santos Emboaba Júnior's goal in the 90th minute could not be considered a "consolation" goal.

Nothing could console the Brazilians after a 7-1 drubbing by Germany. No side had ever lost that badly in a World Cup semi-final.

Brazilians call it the Mineirazo, the Agony of Mineira. Funny that they named it because nobody in Brazil ever, ever speaks of it.

7:1
4

“Agüerooooooooooo...!!!”

There will never be a more dramatic final day of a Premier League season than the one witnessed in 2012.

Going into the beginning of the season, Manchester City had just won their first trophy in 35 years. It seemed the “noisy neighbors” of the most successful club in English history, Manchester United, were beginning to assert their dominance.

Both teams reached the final day of the season level on points.

City had a superior goal difference so it meant that going into the final day of the season they had to beat or match United’s result to be crowned champions of England for the first time in 44 years.

Over in Sunderland, Manchester United beat the hosts - and as the game finished, United players were happy – they heard that City were losing 2-1 at The Etihad in the 90th minute.

There was plenty of injury time to be added on at the City game, and it was during this added time that ‘The Miracle of Manchester’ happened.

In the 92nd minute, Edin Dzeko headed in David Silva’s corner!

At this point, The Red Devil's win over Sunderland still beat a Citizen’s draw. The title was still United’s.

But two minutes is a long time in soccer - and this is all it took for Aguero to take a shot at goal.
The shot rifled into the net and The Etihad went wild.

The commentator of the game howled an incredulous “Agüeroooooooooooooo....” that has now gone down in history as one of the most famous lines in British broadcasting history.

Manchester United were denied a 20th English crown in a cruel fashion, and Agüero forged his name into history books of Manchester City by almost single handedly earning City their first Top flight English crown in 44 years.

The Invincibles

In 2004 Arsenal achieved a feat that had only ever been achieved once before in English Top Flight soccer.

And it's a feat that has not been repeated since: Going a whole season without being defeated.

The only other team to have done it was Preston North End. But they did it in the 1888-1889 season, when it can be argued that it was an easier feat to achieve.

On the back of their unbeaten status, Arsene Wenger's boys won the Premier League in 2004 with 26 wins and a modest (although still impressive) 90 points.

As a result of that magic season, Gunners' fans often reminisce about The Invincibles.

That memorable season saw Thierry Henry lead the way in attack with 30 goals, which ended up being an impressive proportion of the Gunner's total of 73 goals.

Arsenal graced the league in the early noughties with the most exhilarating display of attackers which included Robert Pires, Freddy Ljunberg and Dennis Bergkamp.

Many note, though, that the defense played a huge role. Led by goalkeeper Jens Lehmann, the back line limited the opposition teams to a miserly 26 goals that season.

The truth is that The Invincibles were unbeatable simply because they had quality all over the pitch.

Arsenal went on to lift a special one-off golden edition of the Premier League trophy that season.

The Treble

Liverpool have been there or thereabouts. Manchester City have missed it by a whisker. The Invincibles of 2004 didn't even get near it. It's an almost impossible feat to achieve.

Only one English team has ever won what most consider the most elusive of soccer records: Winning The Premier League, The UEFA Champions League and the Football (soccer) Association Cup in one season.

In 1999, Manchester United did just that. And they did it in one of the most dramatic fashions The Champions League has ever seen.

Having been crowned domestic League and Cup Champions earlier in the month, Manchester United went into the Camp Nou in Barcelona, on the 26th May 1999, knowing that a victory against Bayern Munich would seal their fate as immortals of the game.

They were up against it in Barcelona. And it showed.

For 89 minutes in the final, United players were very average. They were lucky to only be losing 1-0.

But in the 90th minute, David Beckham took a corner. Sheringham scored from it.

In the 92nd minute, Beckham did his thing again and, with literally only a dozen or so seconds left on the clock, Solskjaer scored from Beckham's corner. The most incredible scenes followed.

United had won the Treble in the most dramatic of ways!

Solskjaer ran to the corner and slid on his knees in jubilation. He had just made history.

The world would never see such drama in a final again, until 6 years later in Istanbul when AC Milan and Liverpool met...

The greatest comeback ever

AC Milan were cruising to victory in the UEFA Champions League Final of 2005. They were 3-0 up at half time, and their opponents, Liverpool, were simply outgunned.

As the players trudged back to their dressing rooms, neutral fans couldn't help but feel a sense of embarrassment for the Liverpool players.

What AC Milan had done in the initial 45 minutes was undone in 7 second half minutes by Liverpool.

Captain Steven Gerrard, scored his first headed goal for the club in four years. What a time to break that run. He inspired Vladimir Smicer to score a second two minutes later, before being brought down in the box by Gennaro Gattuso and earning Liverpool a penalty kick. Xabi Alonso tucked it away.

AC Milan capitulated and Liverpool found themselves back in the game.

After a few near misses by AC Milan, the teams found themselves going into a penalty shootout after 120 minutes of soccer played. All was set for the goalkeepers to shine. The Dudek-Dida show.

Dudek most certainly stole the show. Not just because of his dancing antics on the goalline as the opposition lined up to take penalties, but because he saved a penalty from dead ball specialist Andrea Pirlo.

At 3-2 a piece in the penalty shootout, the European Soccer Player Of The Year, Andriy Shevchenko, stepped up. His meek penalty was saved by Dudek and mayhem ensued in Istanbul. Liverpool had just won the trophy after being 3-0 down at half time.

The unlikeliest of comebacks had just taken place. Liverpool gave the world a lesson in grit, determination and perseverance that evening, and sealed a much deserved victory in the Champions League.

Ghana take some time to recover from that!

The first ever World Cup to be hosted in Africa took place in the summer of 2010.

The Ghanaians had a golden generation of a team and they were the undoubted people's favorite as the tournament progressed.

They were seconds away from making it to the semi-final, had it not been for the most dramatic act of dishonesty a World Cup has ever seen.

Ghana and Uruguay were tied at 1-1 and the game went into extra time. In the last minute of extra time, there was a mad scramble in the Uruguayan's box.

In an act of defending desperation, Luis Suarez stopped the Ghanaians from scoring by punching the ball away from his goal line.

For those unfamiliar with the name, Luis Suarez was NOT the Uruguayan goalkeeper. He was Uruguay's striker, and he had just committed the most fragrant and obvious act of cheating the world had ever seen. (What would Paolo Di Canio think?!)

Ghana would have won the game had Suarez not cheated. Instead, they got compensation in the form of a penalty kick.

It was the last kick of the game and they were given the chance to win the game if they scored that penalty kick.

Up stepped Asamoah Gyan who rocketed his shot against the crossbar. Suarez, who was watching from the tunnel (he had been sent off for cheating) celebrated as if he'd just won the World Cup.

It was the most unjust and dramatic quarter final the world had ever seen. The people's champions had been swindled out of a semi-final spot in the first world cup held in their continent.

Ghana went on to lose the game on penalties. Gyan, understandably, was inconsolable after the game. The Uruguayans celebrated wildly into the night.

Seeing red for seeing black

There is a player in Argentina who could well be right in thinking that he's the unluckiest recipient of a red card in the history of the game.

Juan Pablo Krilanovich was playing a game for Lanus Reserves as a midfielder. The tactics were simple from the coach: Apply pressure everywhere on the pitch. Something straight out of the Jurgen Klopp book of coaching.

So when the midfielder was high up the field, applying pressure on the back line of Banfield Reserves, Banfield central defender Lautaro Cardozo panicked.

The age old saying of "when in doubt, kick it out!", came straight to him, and that's exactly what he did. He booted the ball as hard as he could.

Unfortunately for Kirlanovich, he was doing his job of pressing so well (and so quickly!), that his face was right in the way of the defender's clearance.

The ball hit Kirlanovich's face, making him lose consciousness. As a result, his legs stopped functioning properly, and with momentum still in full force, he stumbled towards his opponent.

The midfielder landed awkwardly on the opposition's leg and twisted the defender's knee. Two players out for the count.

One with a suspected twisted knee, and the other with a concussion.

Kirlanovich's concussion didn't last long - he woke up a couple of minutes later and was given a red card by the referee for his clumsy challenge on Cardozo, which unfortunately, did break the defender's leg.

To the best of our knowledge, it's the first red card for an unconscious incident on a soccer pitch.

You can just about hear Kirlanovich's pleading: "But Ref, I was UNCONSCIOUS!"

The Champions League that slipped away

One of the unluckiest moments on a soccer pitch happened on a wet Moscow evening in 2008.

Manchester United and Chelsea had gone head-to-head in the Premier League that season, with United just coming out on top after the last game of the season.

So when the teams met in the final of the Champions League, it couldn't have been a closer affair. The game ended 1-1 and went to penalties. Didier Drogba, one of their main penalty takers, had been sent off in extra time, so he wouldn't have the opportunity to take a penalty.

A very unusual occurrence happened during the shootout: Cristiano Ronaldo missed his penalty. And he missed that penalty in the last game of a season where he had scored 42 goals (including one in that very final!).

It was extremely surprising and unusual. But such is life. The world's best player had, somewhat ironically, cost Manchester United the chance to win the world's biggest club trophy. Or so it seemed...

John Terry stood 12 yards from goal ready to kick into a net only guarded by Edwin Van Der Sar.

Score the penalty and Chelsea win the Champions League. Easy as that.

As John Terry took his kick (Van Der Sar diving the opposite way to the ball), he slipped on the wet Moscow grass and his shot hit the post.

Manchester United not only got back into the shootout but ended up winning the game, lifting the Champions League trophy.

John Terry cut a desolate figure as he left the pitch in tears.

Had Dider Drogba been on the pitch, he probably would have taken the deciding penalty (like he did in Munich 4 years later) and won the game for Chelsea. Without doubt the unluckiest slip of all time.

TERRY

Giants of the game

Soccer tends to be a sport for the quick and flexible, with height being a particular advantage for defenders and strikers.

The game, nonetheless, has had some behemoths on the pitch, men who in other circumstances would have been snapped up as offensive linemen for their local American Football team.

Micky Quinn, born in 1962, was one of those players whose muscular frame eventually ran him into weight issues.

He was, however, a force to be reckoned with, scoring 227 goals in his 535-game professional career.

In his prime, at 88 kg in weight, he was still doing the job. Fans would cheer him on by singing – "He's fat, he's round, he scores at every ground, Micky Quinn, Micky Quinn!"

Opposing fans were less kind, but that did not stop him scoring goals.

However, The King of Timber award in our list of soccer heavies goes to William Foulke.

Foulke, a goalkeeper, filled the goalmouth at 1.9m and 150kg by the end of his professional career.

Foulke won a cap for England in 1897 and played most of his long career for Sheffield United.

He truly was the monster of all monsters, yet surprisingly limber, despite his tonnage.

In fact, he was so limber, that he also played professional cricket during his career!

A Hat-trick of penalty misses!

In 1999 Martin Palermo delivered a performance that defied all odds. It was the group stages of the Copa America, and Argentina were favorites to beat Colombia and top their group.

Five minutes had passed in the game, when a Colombian defender handled the ball in the box. Penalty to Argentina.

Palermo confidently stepped up to the spot and slammed an unstoppable missile into the crossbar – making the ball bounce away into the stands.

It was early. There was plenty of time for it to get worse for Palermo.

Colombia took the lead and shortly after that Argentina got awarded yet another penalty kick.

Funnily enough the same defender handled the ball in the area again. Redemption time for Palermo!

He stepped up and spun the ball into place on the spot. He walked back about half a kilometer, sprinted in and...fired the ball over the crossbar!

With 90 minutes on the clock, Colombia were leading 3-0. The game was well and truly finished, so when Palermo got fouled in the Colombian penalty area and won a penalty kick. He quickly dusted himself off, grabbed the soccer ball and placed it on the spot.

Surely that was the only thing the Argentinians would rescue from the match. Palermo had the chance to atone his two previous penalty misses.

So with arguably the most important thing to play for in his career, his dignity, he took a couple of steps back and took the penalty.

Colombian goalkeeper, Miguel Calero, guessed the direction of the kick and the ball went straight into his midriff. The full time whistle was blown seconds later and Calero joined in the Colombian celebrations!

Palermo is the only holder of this "anti-hat-trick" in soccer, a record three penalties fluffed in an international encounter.

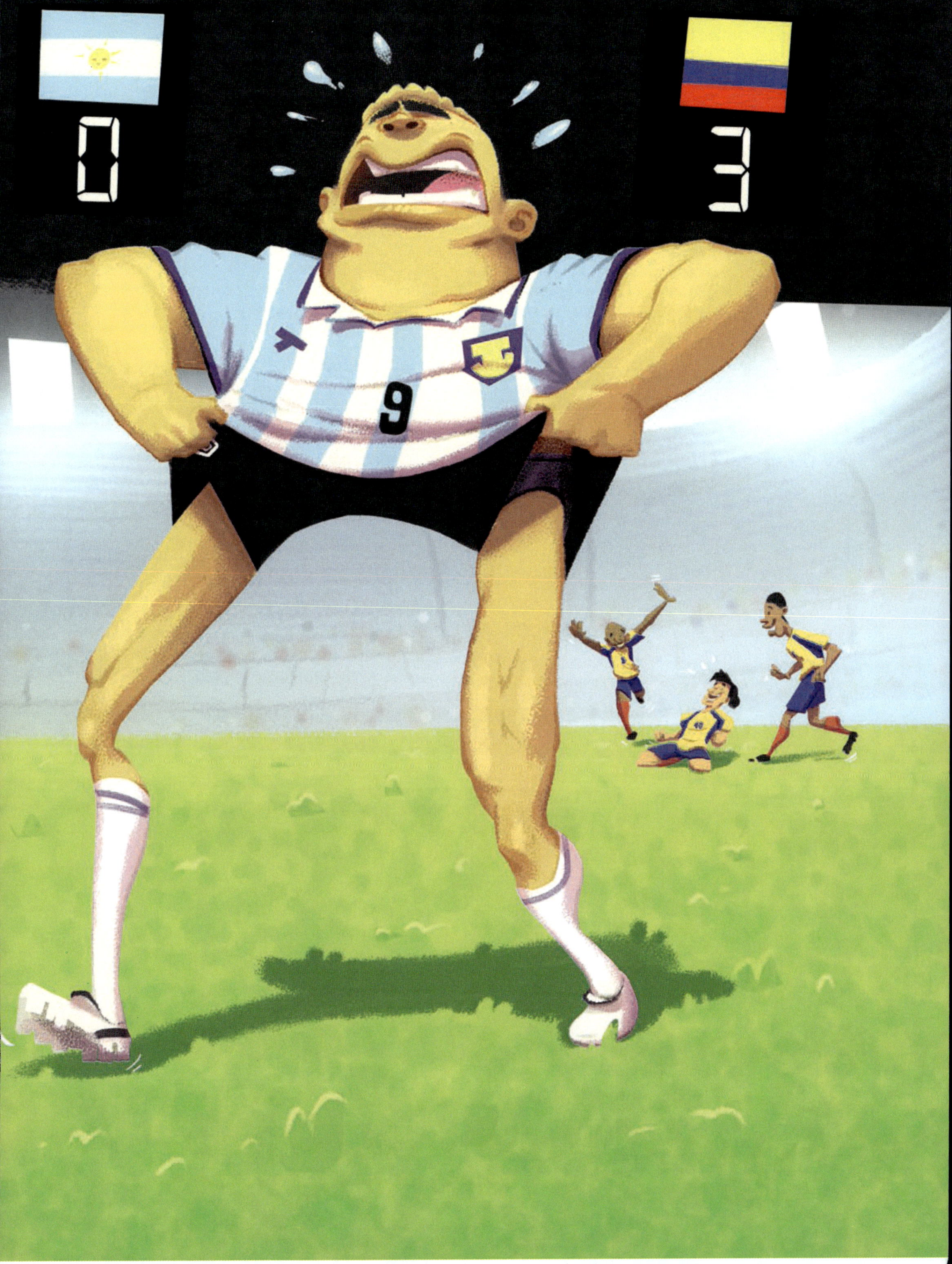
0
3
9

Red card for the ref!

Referee Graham Poll delivered a shocker of a performance in 2006. So much so, that it ended his international whistle-blowing career.

The game was Australia vs Croatia, and in fairness to Poll, he blew an impeccable first half. It was Poll's second half that left a lot to be desired...

In the 61st minute of the game, Croatian defender, Josip Šimunić, was yellow carded for bringing Harry Kewell down in the edge of the box.

The game was tied at 2-2 with a few minutes to go, and things were getting breathless.

Just before stoppage time, Šimunić knocked down an Australian attacker in the area. Poll blew for the penalty and awarded Šimunić another yellow card.

The world stood still, waiting for Poll to show Šimunić the mandatory red that follows two yellow cards... only that never happened!

Poll forgot that Šimunić had been previously booked and failed to send him off. Play continued.

After the game, the referee admitted that he had written the previous yellow card under another player's number in his book, and that's why the second yellow never turned into a red.

As soon as Šimunić realized his luck, you would have thought that he would hide himself away on the field somewhere.

Quite the opposite happened. Šimunić wasn't very good at hiding himself away on the field, and in the 93rd minute, with justice prevailing (or silliness prevailing, it depends on who you ask), Šimunić started arguing with the referee and got booked (for the third time!) for dissent.

Imagine riding your luck that badly that you show dissent after having already been booked twice!

Third time was the charm for Poll, and on that occasion, he rightfully did remember to send the player off!

ŠIMUNOVIĆ
3

He misses more beautifully than others score

When a nice move on the pitch doesn't result in a goal, it is often quickly forgotten. But not in the case of The King, Pelé, who 'scored' the greatest goal that never was.

When he missed the goal, the world took notice. The things he did with his body in the lead up to that miss had never been seen before in the world of soccer.

So how exactly did the most beautiful miss *ever* unfold? It happened in the 1970 World Cup when Brazil were playing Uruguay.

Tostao stole the ball from a Uruguayan player and played a delightful, perfectly weighted through ball to Pelé.

Pelé accelerated towards the ball at the same time as the Uruguayan keeper was. It seemed as if they were both going to get to the ball at exactly the same time.

It seemed inevitable that they were both going to collide on the edge of the box. But in a second that seemed a lifetime, Pelé did nothing but let the ball run past him.

No one does 'nothing' more elegantly than The King. For that split second he danced, played and mesmerized. Danced with the ball, toyed with the keeper, and mesmerized millions.

Pelé's clever maneuver led to the keeper finding himself 25 yards out of his goal, with ZERO clue as to where the ball was. Talk about looking silly!

Pelé knew exactly what he was doing, and without even touching the ball, found himself with an open goal from a tight angle.

He took his shot, and incredibly, the ball trickled a few yards wide from the post.

The game changed that day, however. The greatest miss of all time showed us all that soccer was not a game of brute force, but indeed was The Beautiful Game.

A quick favor

Reviews are the bedrock of my success. Taking 5 minutes of your time to review this book will benefit me in one of two ways.

If the book wasn't to your satisfaction, please leave constructive criticism to make me a better author.

If you enjoyed the book, a good review will give my book more clout in the Amazon algorithms and generate more exposure for my books. I'd be extremely grateful if you could rate my book now.

Thank you.

Instagram: @itsmikelangdon

Made in the USA
Las Vegas, NV
24 August 2023

76545875R00040